THE PRINCIPLES AND PRACTICE OF

ELECTROLOGY

THE PRINCIPLES AND PRACTICE OF

ELECTROLOGY

W.E. Arnould-Taylor M.Sc., Ph.D.

Fellow of The Royal Society of Medicine
Chairman of City and Guilds Working Party on Electrology

in association with

Aileen Harris M.A., M.Phys.

City and Guilds Examiner

Stanley Thornes (Publishers) Ltd.

First published in 1987 by:
Stanley Thornes (Publishers) Ltd
Old Station Drive
Leckhampton
CHELTENHAM GL53 0DN
England

British Library Cataloguing in Publication Data
Arnould-Taylor, W.E.
    The principles and practice of electrology.
    1. Hair—Removal   2. Electrolysis
    I. Title   II. Harris, Aileen
    617'.47   RL115.5

    ISBN 0-85950-577-4

Typeset by Gilbert Composing Services, Leighton Buzzard
in 11/13pt Palatino
Printed and bound in Great Britain at The Bath Press, Avon

Contents

Preface

This textbook first saw the light of day in 1976 as a monograph. Since then there has been a considerably increased interest in the subject of Electrology which is now a compulsory subject in many Beauty Therapy colleges and optional in almost all others. This called for an expanded volume incorporating developments which have taken place in the interim, such as the hot-bead method of sterilisation, and the Government's licensing system for all clinics using invasive techniques. I would like to take this opportunity of acknowledging help which I have received in producing this book, in particular from: Mrs Aileen Harris, who has made valuable contributions; Mr Leo Palladino of the Gloucestershire College of Arts and Technology, for his professional advice on aspects of the content; my colleagues on the City and Guilds Working Party; and my long-time associate, Mrs Kim Aldridge, who encouraged me to write this in the first place.

W.E. Arnould-Taylor
London, 1986

Chapter 1

INTRODUCTION AND HISTORY

It is not the intention of this textbook to deal in very great detail with the vast subject of electrology, but rather to outline the main considerations and to provide the student with all the basic information necessary for the pursuance of a satisfactory electrology practice. It is recognised that this speciality depends for its successful operation on a sympathy for, and an understanding of, people. Extreme patience and an ability to learn from experience is necessary. It is important that this latter consideration should be recognised very early in any course of study. Whilst accurate knowledge is essential, the really successful electrologist is dependent on experience, and this comes only with time and the treatment of a large variety of people.

The history of electrology, as we understand it, is not a very long one, but for a long time people, women in particular, have been conscious of unwanted hair growth, particularly on the face, and down through the ages various methods have been employed to remove undesirable hair. In the 1800s such dangerous practices were used as the application to the skin of sulphuric acid to burn off the hair and the hypodermic injection of phenol (carbolic acid) into the hair follicle. Another method was to tweeze the hair out and then place an unsterilised needle into the hair follicle to produce an inflammation which would eventually seal up the follicular canal. This, it was believed, would completely block the orifice and therefore prevent any hair growing through. These methods were not only largely unsuccessful but were associated with a great deal of pain and a large amount of scarring.

The first record that we have of superfluous hair being removed by electrolytic action was reported in 1875 when Dr. Charles Michel of St. Louis, Missouri, informed members of his own medical profession that he had been able to remove ingrowing eyelashes by the simple method of inserting a needle charged with negative galvanic current into the hair follicle. At this time, the exact action of the galvanic current was not understood and various hypotheses were put forward as to how the hair was destroyed – one of the more picturesque suggestions being that the hair was electrocuted. From then on galvanism was increasingly used for the treatment of unwanted hair, using a single needle. This system, however, was extremely slow and it was not until 1916, when Professor Paul Kree developed the multiple-needle technique, that electrolysis became a practical proposition as a means of removing a large number of hairs. Whereas the single-needle technique took about two minutes to remove one hair, the Kree method enabled four hairs to be removed in the same time. This was, however, basically a galvanic method and therefore still quite slow, and it was destined to be superseded by the now almost universally used diathermic or short-wave method, which is very much faster and less painful.

The tweezer method of epilation (hair removal), whilst slower and apparently much less effective than the needle method, has certain advantages particularly for those people who are frightened of needles.

Most recently we have seen the revival and re-introduction of the 'Blend' machine from the USA. This instrument incorporates the use of both high frequency and galvanic currents simultaneously. In theory it should enable the troublesome deep hair and awkward curved hair follicles to be treated with much more success.

It will be seen, therefore, that the history of electrology in the real sense spans a period of approximately one hundred years but the widespread use of electrology only covers the past thirty years. Today it is universally recognised as a medically approved method of dealing with a problem which, whilst physiological in cause, has wide sociological and psychological repercussions.

It is necessary for aspiring electrologists to have a thorough knowledge of all the aspects covered in this book.

Most of the examining bodies only accept students as Electrology Examination candidates if they have also undertaken a recognised course in Beauty Therapy or in another field of medicine—e.g. nursing. It is therefore considered unnecessary to include chapters in this textbook on neurology, angiology and bacteriology, though aspiring electrologists should have a general knowledge of these.*

*See W.E. Arnould-Taylor, *The Principles and Practice of Physical Therapy*, published jointly by Stanley Thornes (Publishers) Ltd and Arnould-Taylor Education Ltd.

Chapter 2

THE STRUCTURE OF THE SKIN

Although not always recognised as such, the skin is a very large and important organ of the body and it performs many functions for health and beauty. It is an elastic flexible membrane which varies in thickness – being very thin over the eyelids and very thick on the soles of the feet. In an adult it covers about 1.67 square metres.

Friction and pressure tend to increase the thickness of the skin and exposure to warmth and cold strengthens the skin by relaxing and contracting it.

The Stratification of the Skin

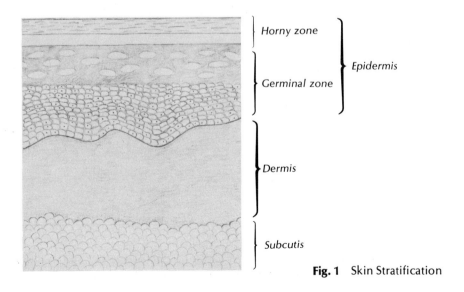

Horny zone

Germinal zone

Epidermis

Dermis

Subcutis

Fig. 1 Skin Stratification

The skin is divided into three layers:

- the **epidermis (cuticle** or **scarf skin);**
- the **dermis (true skin** or **corium);**
- the **subcutis (adipose tissue).**

The Epidermis

There are several layers of cells in the epidermis which extend from the superficial **stratum corneum (horny layer)** to the deepest **germinative layer**. The cells on the surface are flat, thin, non-nucleated dead cells in which the protoplasm has been replaced by a horny substance called **keratin.**

Cells on the surface are constantly being rubbed off and replaced by new cells produced in the germinative layer by a process called **mitosis**, where the cells divide and grow into full-sized cells. They then undergo a gradual change as they progress towards the surface. The maintenance of a healthy epidermis depends on three processes being synchronised:

- desquamation (shedding or peeling) away from the surface of the keratinised cells;
- effective keratinisation (development of a horny quality) of the cells approaching the surface;
- continual cell division (mitosis) in the deeper layers, with the cells being moved upwards towards the surface.

Passing through the epidermis are the hairs, the follicles, and the ducts which carry the secretions of the **sebaceous** and **sudoriferous** (sweat) glands.

The underlying surface of the epidermis, or the lower part of the epidermis, rests on the dermis which is ridged by the projections of dermal cells called the **dermal papillae** (see Fig. 2). The pattern of these ridges formed on the skin of the fingertips is different in every individual. The impressions made by them are called fingerprints, and are now extensively used by the criminologist.

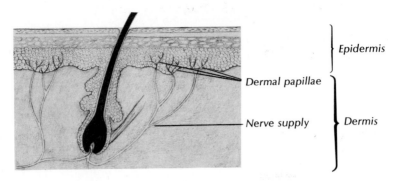

Fig. 2 The Dermal Papillae

The epidermis is divided into two zones:

• the **horny zone**;

• the **germinal zone.**

1 The Horny Zone
This zone is also subdivided into three layers:

(a) Stratum corneum
This is the superficial layer of the skin made up of thin flat cells, the protoplasm of which has been changed into keratin. These cells are constantly being discarded.

(b) Stratum lucidum
The cells in this layer are usually without nuclei and are of an indistinct shape. They allow the light to pass through.

(c) Stratum granulosum
These cells have a distinct shape and contain granules. This layer is believed to be where the cells begin the process of change into keratin.

2 The Germinal Zone
(a) Stratum aculeatum (or mixed-cell layer). This consists of:
(i) Stratum spinosum (or prickle-cell layer)
This is so named because the cells are connected by prickly-looking fibres. These are live cells and have a nucleus.

(ii) Stratum Malpighi (or pigmented layer)
This is also known as the **rete mucosum** or **stratum mucosum**. There are a number of cells in this layer called **melanocytes** which produce the colour pigment of the skin which is called **melanin**. This varies in different races throughout the world. Melanin helps to protect the skin from the harmful ultraviolet rays of the sun and sun lamps, and is actively involved in skin tanning. An absence of melanin produces a condition called **albinism**, when the skin and hair are pinkish-white, the eyes are pink and vision is poor.

(b) Stratum germinativum or stratum basale
This is the base, or germinating layer, of the epidermis. It is the level where mitosis takes place. The cells spend about six weeks in this layer before becoming flattened and passing upwards to the stratum corneum, or horny layer, of the skin.

N.B. In some textbooks the layers described above are regarded as one.

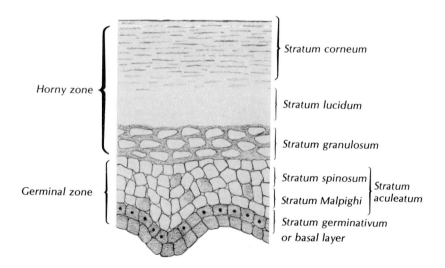

Fig. 3 The Epidermis

The Dermis

The dermis is sometimes called the **true skin**. It is a tough, flexible mixture of elastic connective tissue, in which the fibres are irregularly orientated.

It is divided into two layers (see Fig. 4):

- the **papillary layer;**
- the **reticular layer.**

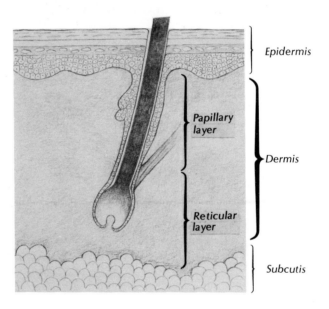

Fig. 4 The Dermal Layers

1 The Papillary Layer

This consists of closely intermeshed elastic fibres which are collagenous, i.e. they resemble albumen (egg white). Papillae bear numerous nerve endings and as well as being profusely vascular they project themselves into the epidermis causing, as we have already mentioned, the irregular pattern of finger-prints on the surface of the epidermis. It is from this layer that the sense of touch is derived and from which the dermis and the lower levels of the epidermis receive their blood supply.

2 The Reticular Layer

This is a looser weave of collagenous and elastic fibres, and it may contain considerable adipose tissue so that its transition into the subcutaneous layer below is not always clearly demarcated.

This layer also contains:

(a) Capillary blood vessels
A fine network of capillaries carries oxygen and nutrients to the skin. Deoxygenated blood is returned to the lungs by a network of venules which joins the main venous system. The blood is then oxygenated and pumped by the heart through a system of arteries back to the skin and other parts of the body.

(b) Lymphatic vessels
These vessels dispose of the waste materials and toxins.

(c) Sensory and motor nerve endings
Sensory (**afferent**) nerve fibres carry sensory messages to the spinal cord and then to the brain from specialised receptor organs located throughout the dermis giving the sense of heat, cold, pain and touch. Motor (**efferent**) fibres convey impulses from a nerve centre to regulate contraction of the smooth muscles as well as regulating sweat glands, etc.

(d) The sudoriferous glands
These are tubular organs which extend from a coiled end in the dermis to open on the surface of the epidermis as pores. These glands help to control the temperature of the body and to eliminate waste materials. There are two types of sudoriferous gland:

(i) Apocrine glands
These larger glands are located in special places throughout the body, e.g. the axillae, groin and scalp, as they are mainly connected to the hair follicles. They secrete sweat and excrete waste, salt and water.

(ii) Eccrine glands

These smaller glands are found in large numbers all over the body. They produce sweat within the main body of the gland which is secreted out on to the skin surface.

The products of both apocrine and eccrine glands contribute to body odour if not regularly cleansed from the skin.

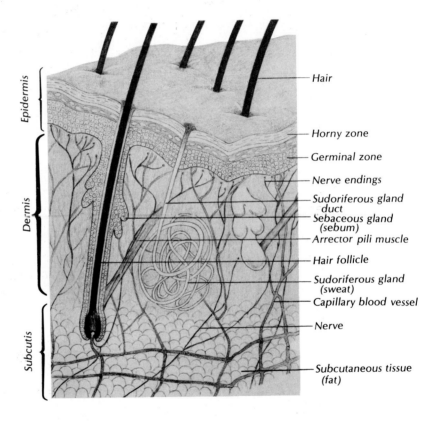

Fig. 5   Skin Stratification and Appendages

(e) The sebaceous glands

With a few exceptions, the sebaceous glands are connected to the hair follicles as they develop from the follicular epithelium of the hair. They are variable in size and are either simple or multilobed structures which empty their short ducts directly into the hair follicle.

The glands produce an oily secretion called **sebum**, which forms the greater part of the lipid (fat) component of the surface film over the skin and also lubricates the hair to keep it soft. An excess production of sebum can make the hair and skin appear oily. If it is allowed to accumulate and oxidise it may contribute to disorders of the skin, e.g. acne and blackheads. Too little sebum produced results in dry skin and brittle hair.

(f) The hair and the hair follicle
A hair is a horny, elastic, thread-like structure derived from the epidermis. Hair is found all over the body, except on the lips, the hands and the soles of the feet. The part of the hair above the surface is called the **shaft**. The **hair bulb** is found at the lower end of the hair and is embedded in the dermis. The bulb surrounds an area called the **papilla** which is not directly part of the hair. The papilla consists of blood vessels which supply the nutrients to activate the **germinal matrix**, a cellular zone lining the underside of the hair bulb (see Fig. 6).

The hair follicle can be regarded as an indentation in the skin, and the hair, the follicle and the sebaceous gland are referred to as the **pilosebaceous unit.**

The Subcutis

This layer contains bundles of connective tissue, fat cells, the large blood vessels to the skin, the lymph vessels, the heavier nerve trunks and the specialised deep pressure receptors (**Pacinian corpuscles**). It is always a target for fat in overweight conditions, especially in certain areas, such as the back of the arm, the midriff, the abdomen, the hips, the thighs and the buttocks.

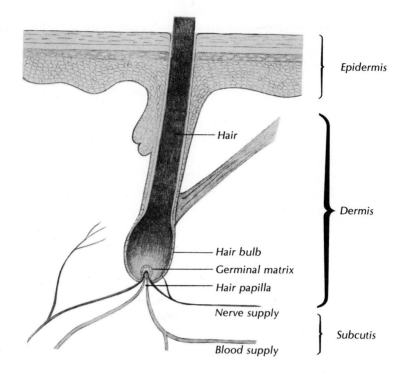

Epidermis

Hair

Dermis

Hair bulb
Germinal matrix
Hair papilla
Nerve supply

Subcutis

Blood supply

Fig. 6 The Germinal Matrix

The Functions of the Skin

The skin performs a variety of important functions:

- **Protection:** It serves as a protective covering for the body and its other organs and is impervious to most germs and infections except where it is broken.

- **Heat regulation:** It regulates the body temperature so that when the internal heat of the body rises above its norm (36.8 °C or 98.4 °F), the excess heat is eliminated by means of the skin either in the form of radiation or perspiration.

- **Sensation:** It provides the body with one of its largest areas of sensation, as most of the sensory nerve endings (heat, cold, pain, touch and pressure) terminate in the skin.

- **Absorption:** The skin, because of its oily particles, is capable of absorbing oily substances but not water.
- **Secretion:** The sebaceous glands secrete sebum which keeps the skin and hair soft and pliable. Sebum assists in producing the acid mantle over the skin which helps to protect it.
- **Elimination:** The sudoriferous glands eliminate waste materials by perspiration and also prevent the amount of water loss from being excessive and thus drying out the tissues.
- **The formation of vitamin D:** There is a fatty substance called **ergosterol** in the skin which the ultraviolet light converts into vitamin D. The vitamin D circulates in the blood and is used with calcium and phosphorus in the formation and maintenance of bone. Excess vitamin D is stored in the liver.

The Recognition of Various Skin Types

From the study of Beauty Therapy we are aware that skin types fall into certain categories, i.e. normal, dry, oily, and combination. But within these categories there are many variations, for instance in sensitivity, moisture content, thickness, pigmentation and softness.

For the purpose of electrology the operator should note whether or not the client has:

- moist skin
- thin skin
- soft skin
- sensitive skin
- oily skin

The machine setting and the depth of needle insertion are governed by the skin type, and they may affect the efficiency of the treatment.

Common Conditions and Disorders

The following are some of the conditions and disorders that an electrologist might encounter during the course of treatment applications.

Eyes

Cataracts
The lens of the eye is situated directly behind the pupil and in health is clear. With age, and in some diseases such as diabetes, it loses its transparency and becomes more and more opaque, gradually shutting out vision. This condition is known as a cataract. It is not a growth but a biochemical change in the lens.

Conjunctivitis
This is inflammation of the conjunctiva – the mucous membrane of the eye. In its acute, contagious form it is known as 'pink eye'. It may be caused by various forms of bacteria and virus infections. There is a 'swimming-bath' conjunctivitis and a type which develops as a result of exposure to ultra-violet rays.

Stye *(hordeolum)*
A stye is usually caused by bacteria invading one or more eyelash follicles where infection takes place. If, on the other hand, the small sweat glands of the eyelid are infected a cyst or chalazion forms.

Eyelid Inflammation *(blepharitis)*
Inflammation of the eyelids is due to the infection of the small sebaceous glands. It may be caused by rubbing, scratching or an allergic reaction which affects mainly the eyelids. It is more commonly caused by bacterial infection of the eyelash follicle and glands.

Face

Common Acne (acne vulgaris)
This is one of the most common forms of skin disease. It is
due to the oversecretion of the sebaceous glands invariably
associated with an increase of hormones prevalent at puberty
in both male and female. The primary lesion is the raised,
pus-filled spot or pustule, usually accompanied by comedones
or blackheads. Suppuration (discharge of pus), inflammation
and scarring are common.

Blackheads (comedo)
These are small, dark plugs of oxidised sebum which block
the skin pores, the follicle opening and the sebaceous ducts.
The hardened substance is darkened by exposure to the air
rather than dirt. Blackheads may contain harmless parasites.

Whiteheads (milia)
These are small, pearly white nodules which occur commonly in dry skin around the eyes. They are usually caused by
small amounts of trapped sebum in a sebaceous duct without
an opening. They may also be caused by other trapped kera-
tinous matter which forms tiny cysts in the skin.

Freckles (ephelides)
These are small, brown areas of various shapes, distributed
in any part of the skin surface. They appear to be common
in redheads and fair skins and are due either to large numbers of grouped melanocytes – the cells which produce the
colour pigment of the skin – or to an increased amount of
melanin in the skin. They are commonly found on exposed
areas of the body, e.g. face, neck, arms and legs.

Cold Sore (herpes simplex)
This is a viral infection of the skin which is characterised by
initial irritation, often about the lips, inflammation, soreness
and the formation of vesicles, or blisters filled with blood or
pus. The areas affected vary, but sores around the mouth
and nose are common. A cold sore clears after a day or two

and does not usually leave any skin defects. The virus is situated in the skin, sometimes for years, until it is triggered to erupt.

Scalp and Head

Areas of Baldness *(alopecia areata)*
In this condition, hair is lost in circumscribed areas of the scalp or beard. There is no obvious sign of skin disorder or systemic disease. The area of baldness is usually pale and shiny with an absence of irritation or inflammation. Hair shaped like an exclamation mark at the margins of the bald patches is characteristic. Initial hair loss may be rapid; several areas of baldness may occur simultaneously, and join together to produce *alopecia totalis* – complete baldness of the head. If all the hair of the body is lost the term *alopecia universalis* is given to the condition.

Scalp Ringworm *(tinea capitis)*
This is a fungal infection of the hair and scalp. It commonly occurs, in both the male and female, before puberty. It is characterised by partial hair loss due to the hair breaking off in the areas attacked by the fungus. It is spread by direct contact with an infected person, or through the use of head-gear, combs, or brushes of an infected person. A red, inflamed ring of fungal activity can be distinctly seen surrounding an area of broken hairs. Ringworm of the body *(tinea corporis)* often exhibits the characteristic red ring more clearly. In ringworm of the nails *(tinea ungulum)* the nails become discoloured, horny and disfigured. The disease may also take the form of ringworm of the feet *(tinea pedis)*, commonly called athlete's foot.

A variety of fungi are responsible for types of *tinea* which attack specific parts of the body.

Dandruff *(pityriasis capitis* or *pityriasis sicca)*
Small, dry, flaking scales of the epidermis give rise to this condition. It is usually accompanied by irritation of either localised areas or the whole scalp. The condition may be

caused by physiological, mechanical or chemical irritants which increase normal skin shedding and normal cell production. There may be fungal and bacterial infections which add further to the irritation of cell division and shedding. If it remains untreated more complicated skin conditions may result. Dandruff may be treated with special shampoos particularly those containing zinc pyrithione.

Skin Generally

Psoriasis
This is a non-infectious skin condition due mainly to an abnormal epidermal cell formation which accumulates at the skin surface. It is estimated that psoriasis may affect 5–6 per cent of the population. It occurs in families and about 25 per cent of cases are thought to be due to an inherited tendency towards the condition. The characteristic lesion is a raised, thickened area of skin, slightly white or silvery and sometimes red at the margins. In the scalp the scales tend to build up due to the hair. In some there is intense irritation, while others experience no itching at all. The condition may become more active at specific times of the year according to the individual and appears to be aggravated by stress and tension. It may occur on the fingernails, toenails and commonly on the scalp.

Eczema
Eczema is a term now used synonymously with dermatitis. It is, in the early stages, an inflammation of the skin, but it may quickly develop into a number of different states until complete breakdown of the skin occurs. Both internal and external factors may be involved. Some reactions are due to allergic response to some foods, while others are due to external chemical, physical and pathological irritants. Eczema is recognised by the varying degrees of inflammation with which it is associated. Swelling may be present. Small vesicles may form which tend to merge to form larger areas. Weeping and crusting can develop, followed by pigmentation and thickening of the skin. A burning sensation and irritation

are usually felt. Common examples of this condition are: contact dermatitis derived from wearing lipstick and perfume; housewife's hands due to excessive use of detergents; industrial dermatitis due to many of the oils and materials used; and infantile eczema due to skin dryness, chafing or allergic reaction.

Shingles *(herpes zoster)*

Shingles is a viral infection of the skin and the nerve endings of the skin. It is associated with people who have previously suffered from chicken pox and, like herpes simplex, it may lie dormant in the skin for many years. Small vesicles may appear. Fever, inflammation and areas of sore skin can develop before any lesion appears. There may be swelling and enlargement of the glands, and severe pain and scarring can occur.

Colourless Skin *(vitiligo* or *leucodermia)*

This is a condition of the skin where colour has been lost, or where the normal process of pigmentation has failed to deposit or evenly distribute the melanin necessary for normal skin colour. The darker the surrounding skin colour, the more obvious is the condition. Smooth, white, clearly defined areas of skin are commonly seen on the neck and face, but may appear anywhere on the body. The patches are irregular and without scaling or any other lesion. They may merge to form larger areas of depigmented skin. Repigmentation may occur naturally after a number of years but remedial skin camouflage offers the most satisfactory and speedy assistance for those suffering from this condition.

Moles *(naevi)*

These are heavily pigmented areas of skin which take various forms and shapes. They may be first seen soon after birth and can disappear later in life. Some are flat, smooth, round or irregular in shape and dark in colour. Others may be pale-to-brown raised lesions and are commonly seen on the face and body. **Papilloma** is the term given to the warty type of mole. The hairy mole *(naevus pilosis)* is usually pigmented and, as its name suggests, endowed with strong hairs.

Keloids

These are fibrous tumours of the dermis which usually occur
on the sites of injuries or old scars. They may also form
around ingrowing hairs. *Acne keloid* or *sycosis nuchae* are the
names given to keloids which form around pustular lesions
of acne. These characteristic lesions may be recognised by
the presence of red, white or purplish, hard ridges of irregularly shaped scar-like tissue. The skin becomes very hard,
shiny and raised. Keloids are commonly found on the neck.

Warts *(verrucae)*

Warts are viral infections of the skin which occur in a
variety of shapes, sizes and colours. They may be flat, raised,
stalked, rough, smooth, or pearly, and may occur singly or in
clusters. Some irritate and most bleed when torn or cut.
Common warts *(verrucae vulgaris)* are often found on the
hands and face. Many are brown and may be mistaken for
small *naevi*. The plane wart *(verruca plana)* is a viral tumour of
the skin. It is a small, slightly raised or flat papule, which
may seem to have a smooth surface, and is commonly found
in children. The plantar wart *(verruca plantar)* is another type
of viral skin tumour. It lies in, rather than on, the skin and
is commonly found on the heel or sole of the foot. Small
black specks may be visible in plantar warts; and irritation or
inflammation results in pain and discomfort. The senile wart
(verruca senilis) is associated with ageing skin and is not a viral
infection. Senile warts may appear singly or in groups. At
first lightly coloured they may later become heavily pigmented. They are small, soft, smooth, and rub off easily, and
they are usually accompanied by itching.

The above list of disorders is by no means an exhaustive
one. There are several infectious conditions of the skin with
which the professional electrologist should be familiar. Further study is indicated. Treatment must not be carried out
by the electrologist where there are signs of infectious conditions. These clients must be referred to their doctors for
advice and guidance.

Chapter 3

THE STRUCTURE OF HAIR

Hairs are dead keratinised structures. The hair follicle is a tube-like indentation lined with epidermis which extends from the surface downwards to various depths of the dermis and subcutis according to the stage of growth and type of hair it contains.

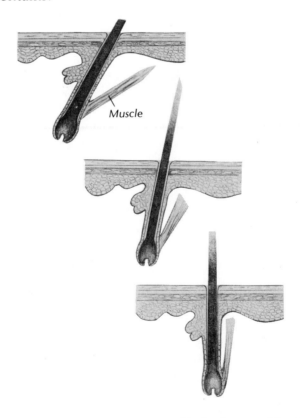

Muscle

Fig. 7   Arrector Muscle Contraction

The hair and follicle are situated in the skin at a slanting angle which varies in each individual and differs between follicles in the same skin. When the hair muscle *(arrector pili)* contracts, the hair and follicle become erect and the hair stands upright from the skin (see Fig. 7). This usually occurs when fear is experienced, and is displayed, for example, by a cat when threatened with attack from another animal. This is part of the protective function of the hair. It also occurs when the skin is cold—muscle contraction produces the characteristic 'goose pimples'. This is part of the protective response against heat loss.

The most important part of the structure as regards growth of hair and regeneration of the follicle is at the papilla and germinal matrix of the hair bulb situated in the dermis.

Hair Types

Hair undergoes changes throughout the life of the body and three particular types are recognised.

1 Lanugo Hair
Lanugo hair is the hair of the unborn child and the first result of cellular activity in the skin. It is fine, fluffy hair which is usually discarded before, or soon after, birth and replaced by hair which, though still fine, is slightly coarser.

2 Vellus Hair
Vellus hair is soft, downy, fine and fluffy. It covers most of the skin in much the same way as on a peach, and grows from a shallow depth in the skin. It is to be found on the cheeks of females and the bald heads of males, and appears to be a coarser type of lanugo hair which finally develops into terminal hair.

3   Terminal Hair

Terminal hair is thick, coarse hair which grows to longer lengths then vellus hair and from a greater depth in the skin. It is usually abundant on the male chest and beard, on the scalp, under the arms, in the pubic areas and in other parts of the body.

Terminal hairs on the body take different forms and shapes. Long terminal hairs of the scalp differ from those of the beard and legs. The eyelashes and eyebrows are shorter and distinctive and have adapted to the different functions that they fulfil. Unlike other follicles the eyelash follicle is not angled in the skin – it is upright in the skin, which causes the eyelash to project straight out. The orifices of the body such as the ears and nostrils, have their own type of protective, shaped hairs.

Hair is given different names in different parts of the body, as follows: head, *capilli*; eyelashes, *cilia*; nostrils, *vibrissae*; ears, *tragi*; eyebrows, *supercilia*; face, *barba*; armpits, *hirci*; pubic region, *pubes*.

The Hair

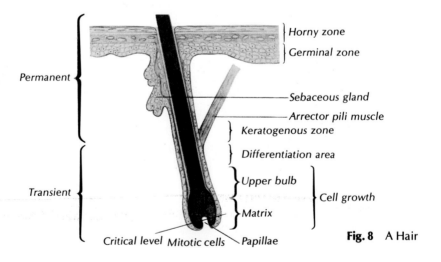

Fig. 8   A Hair

The cells of which hair is composed are arranged in three layers.

1 The Cuticle or Outer Horny Layer
This is made of fine scales which overlap each other and it provides the hair with its elasticity.

2 The Cortex
This layer is made of elongated cells, and melanin granules in these cells cause the pigmentation of the hair.

3 The Medulla
The centre area of the hair has loosely connected keratinised cells interspersed with airspaces, which create the colour tones by influencing the reflection of light.

The Structure of the Hair Follicle

The follicle comprises three layers:

- the **inner root sheath;**
- the **outer root sheath;**
- the **connective tissue sheath.**

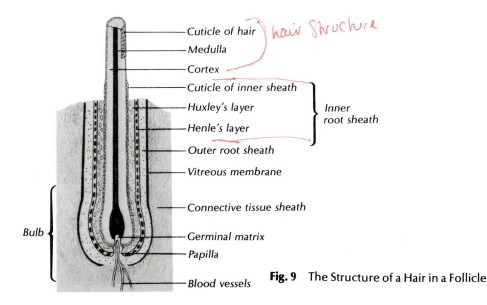

Cuticle of hair
Medulla
Cortex
Cuticle of inner sheath
Huxley's layer
Henle's layer
Inner root sheath
Outer root sheath
Vitreous membrane
Connective tissue sheath
Bulb
Germinal matrix
Papilla
Blood vessels

Fig. 9 The Structure of a Hair in a Follicle

The Inner Root Sheath

This is composed of:

- The cuticle layer which holds the cuticle of the hair;
- **Huxley's layer** – the thickest layer;
- **Henle's layer.**

N.B. There are two layers which are called the cuticle:

- the cuticle layer of the hair;
- the cuticle layer of the inner root sheath.

Both layers have scale-like cells and they lock together holding the hair firmly in place (see Fig. 10).

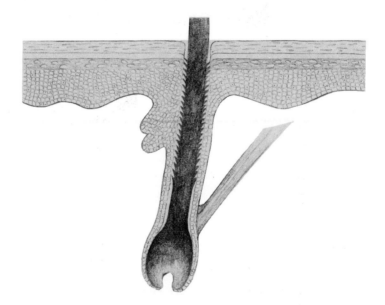

Fig. 10   The Hair and Follicle Cuticles Interlocking

The cellular growth of the inner root sheath and the hair begins at the lowest part of the follicle at the papilla. They grow upwards together as far as the sebaceous gland where the inner root sheath disappears and the hair continues upwards until it reaches the cavity in the epidermis.

The Outer Root Sheath

This surrounds the inner root sheath and is of uneven thickness, which causes the hair to be eccentric in the hair follicle. The outer root sheath remains stationary rather than growing upwards, but the cellular structure of the outer root sheath cannot be distinguished from that of the surface epidermis at the level of the sebaceous gland and above, and the follicle is therefore called an indentation of the epidermis.

The outer root sheath is of particular interest to electrologists as they can use the moisture content, which is water-soluble animal starch glycogen, to attract the electrical current. This sheath also has hair germ cells which can be stimulated by hormones and enzymes to produce new hair follicles. It is regarded as a continuation of the **stratum Malpighi** and the **stratum germinativum** of the epidermis.

The Connective Tissue Sheath

The papillary layer of the dermis supplies blood and nerve endings for the hair follicle and the sebaceous glands. The connective tissue sheath, which surrounds the follicle and the glands, is like an extension of the papillary layer of the dermis and it contains the dermal papilla itself, which is responsible for the structure of the hair follicle.

The Stages of Hair Growth

There are three stages in the growth of a hair which an electrologist should understand (see Fig. 11):

- **anagen;**
- **catagen;**
- **telogen.**

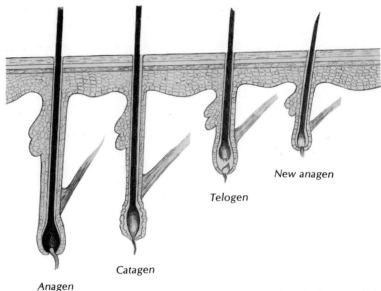

New anagen

Telogen

Catagen

Anagen

Fig. 11   Stages of Hair Growth

Anagen

Anagen is the time when the follicle comes to life and grows with nourishment from the dermal papilla. After the resting or telogen period in the cycle of growth (see opposite page), the hair germ cells extend downwards from the existing follicle in a cord called the dermal cord, which multiplies its cell structure by mitosis and grows in width and depth. The dermal cord meets and surrounds the basic papilla cells which become the papilla, and the cord itself becomes the bulb.

Before the follicle ceases its downward journey, the mitotic cells in the lower part of the bulb (called the matrix) begin to produce the constituent elements of the hair and the inner root sheath. In the upper part of the bulb the cells are keratinised and forced up through the cord forming the inner root sheath and the hair. The hair follows the sheath, breaking through the centre of the permanent upper hair follicle. When the hair has grown to about 1 cm above the epidermis, the follicle ceases to grow downwards.

There are four regions of specialised activity in the growth of the hair (see Fig. 8):

- below the matrix – mitotic cells;
- the upper bulb – the growth and elongation of the cells;
- the differentiation area – the cells change into the soft, three-layered structure of mature hair;
- the keratogenous zone – the complete hair emerges.

Catagen

During this stage it appears that the dermal papilla detaches itself from the matrix and ceases to nourish the follicle. The follicle then shrinks upwards, but the hair is still nourished by elements in the follicle walls. The undifferentiated cells again become the dermal cord. Slowly the hair is detached and is shed, or on occasion remains dormant – its **club** root remains in the upper follicle. Sometimes the follicle is reformed so quickly that there are two hairs in the follicle.

Telogen

This is a period when the upper portion of the hair follicle usually rests, and when all that remains below this part of the follicle is a collection of hair germ cells from the outer root sheath and the dermal papilla cells. These cells are the basic units from which new follicles will grow. The period of resting varies.

N.B. It is important for the electrologist to destroy the hair germ cells and the dermal cells as well as the papilla, which is generally believed to be all-important.

Chapter 4

THE CAUSES OF HAIR GROWTH

It is important to understand the following terms relating to the growth of hair:

- **Superfluous hair:** hair which is not considered unnatural, but which is not acceptable socially, e.g. hair appearing at certain stages of life, such as the menopause;

- **Hypertrichosis:** growth of hair on any part of the body in excess of that which is considered to be natural;

- **Hirsutism:** growth of hair in excess of that which is considered natural, but usually following the pattern of the growth of male sexual hair and sometimes including the back and the shoulders.

New hair growth is caused by stimulation to the hair germ cells or dermal cells by either:

- an increase in the supply of blood, or
- hormone stimulation

An increase in the blood supply accelerates the growth of already existing hair, e.g. vellus, but it will not create new hairs. On the other hand, certain hormones cause new hairs to spring from the hair germ cells near the sebaceous glands. The increased supply of blood to moles and birthmarks often causes thick bristles to come from these areas. Electrologists are advised not to tamper with these areas. It used to be thought that electrology could cause these areas to become cancerous. No evidence is available to prove this theory, but most insurance companies specify that moles, warts and unusual circumstances which might cause hair growth, should be avoided when applying treatments.

It is generally recognised that the basic causes of hair growth may be divided into four categories:

- congenital causes;
- topical causes;
- systemic causes;
- pathological disorders.

Congenital Causes

In considering congenital causes, we must, of course, take into account the variations in ethnic groups. In general, Anglo-Saxon and Nordic strains (British, Germanic and Scandinavian) are less hairy than the Mediterranean and Semitic peoples, white-skinned people are usually more hairy than negro types, and the least hairy of all are Mongolians and Orientals. The general pattern of hair growth, therefore, is one of heredity, the genetic factors being provided by the father and mother. But these genetic factors have, in turn, been influenced by topical causes (see below), and translated in evolutionary terms into congenital ones.

Topical Causes

It has already been seen that hair receives its nourishment from the blood supply. Plucking or sustained irritation will result in an increased blood supply to the area, but, at the same time, will stimulate the hairs in order to provide a covering to protect the skin against further irritation. It is the protective function of hair which is the evolutionary cause of the heavy growth of hair in particular parts of the body. Hair on the head is a protection against the effects of the sun, or of concussion in the case of a fall or bump; hair in the armpits is a protection against constant friction; and pubic hair is a cushion during intercourse. Almost any form of physical irritation on the surface of the skin will produce hair, but in many cases these are fine hairs which disappear fairly soon after the cause of the irritation has been removed. Perhaps the most common instance of this is to be found in limbs which have been kept in plaster for several months, and where the constant chafing has caused a protective covering to appear, but it can also arise as a result of X-rays, too much ultraviolet light and even constant scratching.

Tweezing is a very good example of the type of irritation which accelerates growth. When a hair is tweezed out of its follicle, a good deal of the bottom of the follicle is torn out. Whilst this damage is not sufficient to prevent further growth, it is enough for the follicle to reconstruct itself in such a way that it is a little sturdier and better able to deal with the next onset. Whilst tweezing therefore tends to make the hair grow more sturdily, shaving would appear to have no such effect – despite the common belief that it has.

Tests have also been carried out involving shaving various parts of the body. These have been conducted on both sexes over a longish period of time. No differences have been found in the amount, length, diameter or pigmentation of the hairs on the shaved areas as compared with the hairs on the unshaved areas of the same person. It will be noted that shaving does not cause an irritation – it only cuts off the hair at the surface and does nothing to injure the follicle.

Systemic Causes

Glands are known to play a very important part in hair growth, as is evidenced when the glands are particularly active, in puberty, pregnancy and menopause. It is not appropriate here to go into a long and detailed account of all the glands which secrete hormones into the blood, but rather to point out the part played by the adrenal cortex. The adrenal glands, which are sometimes called the supra-renals, are situated one above each kidney. Each adrenal gland has two parts – the medulla and the cortex. The medulla produces adrenaline (epinephrine), which is sometimes referred to as the 'fight or flight' hormone.

The adrenal cortex, on the other hand, produces hormones called steroids. There are more than thirty of these known to science but they may be divided into two groups – the cortico-steroids and the sex hormones. It is the sex hormones which primarily interest us here: **androgens** (the male hormones) and **oestrogens** and **progesterone** (the female hormones).

The presence of the adrenal cortex means that every person carries a combination of both sexes as far as this hormone potential is concerned, and it is the predominance of one set of hormones over the other which determines sex character-istics. The important thing to remember about the adrenal glands is that in both male and female they are a source of androgens, and androgens are capable of stimulating face and body hair – a fact which is evident at puberty, when both underarm and pubic hair develop in males and females. It will therefore be readily seen that an imbalance between the androgens, oestrogens and progesterone can result in increased unwanted hair in females. It will also be noted that certain drugs which contain hormones, such as cortisone and contraceptive pills, may also lead to abnormal hair growth. Stress can also be responsible for increased hair growth because of the increased adrenaline which it produces. Another factor which may affect hair growth is surgical intervention, e.g. the removal of the ovaries, which produces a kind of artificial menopause with much the same results.

Pathological Disorders

N.B. Any client suffering from an obvious disorder should be advised to see her doctor.

There are several pathological disorders causing hypertrichosis and hirsutism about which the electrologist should have a back-ground knowledge.

Cushing's Syndrome

This disease is usually characterised by:

- obesity of the face, neck and trunk, but limbs remaining unaffected;
- ceasing of menstruation in women;
- roundness of the shoulders;
- a darkening of the skin and an increased tendency towards bruising;
- an abnormal amount of hair growth.

The syndrome may be caused by: any prolonged medication which stimulates the adrenal cortex to produce an excessive amount of hormones including androgens; an excessive development of cells in the adrenal cortex; and the presence of tumours in the cortex or pituitary gland.

Adrenogenital Syndrome

This is usually caused by a tumour or an abnormality in the adrenal cortex. The adrenal cortex cannot use the chemical materials needed for manufacturing cortisones, but produces androgens instead. Girls are affected by their external genitalia tending to become masculine, and they may develop a beard, a moustache and a deep voice. Boys become very sexually developed, with all the secondary characteristics associated with puberty.

Achard-Thiers Syndrome

This combines the symptoms of both of the previous syndromes, and is also known as 'diabetes of the bearded woman'.

Stein-Leventhal Syndrome

Women suffer from either excessive uterine bleeding or lack of menstruation. Hirsutism is frequent, occasionally there is no

breast development, and obesity often accompanies the condition. The development of ovarian cysts is thought to relate to
the cause of this syndrome.

Acromegaly

This is usually caused by a growth in the pituitary gland. It
causes gigantism, which is usually most marked on the face,
hands and feet, and it can also affect vision by the pressure of
the enlargement of various areas. Acromegaly also produces an
excessive hair growth on the face.

Chapter 5

TREATMENT METHODS

The Use of Electrical Equipment

The principles of electricity have already been dealt with in the author's book, *The Principles and Practice of Physical Therapy*, and it is therefore not deemed appropriate to deal with them in detail here, but rather to concentrate on those considerations which are of primary concern to the electrologist. For the convenience of the reader, the following outline of some electrical points might serve as a useful guide.

Electrical equipment designed for use in Britain is based on the mains supply which is 240 volts. In the rest of Europe it is generally 110 volts. Some equipment may be suitable for use on both 240 and 110 volts. Before purchasing or using, always check that the equipment suits the voltage available to prevent damage occurring.

Electrical Units

Unit of electrical current   — amp (A)
Unit of electrical potential   — volt (V)
Unit of electrical power   — watt (W)
Unit of electrical resistance — ohm
One kilowatt (kW)   — 1000 watts
One kilowatt hour (kWh) — work done by 1 kW in 1 hour

The relationship between the electrical units may be expressed by the following examples:

To find the correct fuse for a piece of equipment

$$\frac{watts}{volts} = amps$$ The wattage divided by the voltage gives the size of amperage fuse required.

e.g. a piece of equipment using 1000 watts on a voltage of 240 will require the following fuse size:

$$\frac{1000}{240} = 4.2 \text{ amps}$$ Therefore a fuse (nearest size) of 5 amps will be required.

To make sure that the system is not overloaded it is possible to calculate the maximum amount of equipment that can be used at the same time.

volts × amps = watts

e.g. a 13-amp-fused socket on a 240 voltage will take 240 volts × 13 amps = 3120 watts maximum can be used.

More than this will 'blow' the fuse. The amount of watts used by equipment is usually marked on a plate at the back.

To calculate the cost of running electrical equipment
add the total wattage of the equipment being used;
divide by 1000 to arrive at the number of kilowatts;
multiply by the number of hours equipment is used;
multiply by the rate per unit.

e.g. $\frac{3000}{1000}$ watts   = 3 kilowatts

used for four hours = 3 × 4 = 12

at 5p per kWh   = 12 units at 5p per unit

                                = 60p

Therefore it costs 60p to run 3000 watts for four hours.

Fuse Sizes

The following sizes of fuse will take up to the following amounts of wattage before becoming overloaded and 'blowing' or melting.

1 amp — 240 watts
2 amp — 480 watts
3 amps — 720 watts
5 amps — 1200 watts

10 amps — 2400 watts
13 amps — 3120 watts
20 amps — 4800 watts
30 amps — 7200 watts

Precautions

It is important that electrical equipment is handled with extreme care, and the following points should be observed.

- Equipment should be switched off and unplugged from the socket when not in use.

- Avoid using adaptors in sockets.

- Do not use damaged plugs.

- Any doubt about a piece of equipment should be reported and a qualified electrician should deal with problems arising.

- Do not pull on cables to remove plugs from sockets.

- Cables exposed to excessive heat can become damaged and dangerous.

- Trailing cables are a hazard and must be avoided.

- Always check voltage and correct fusing of new equipment.

- If a fuse overheats, switch off immediately and check the appliance. Faults must be corrected before using again.

- All electrical equipment must be regularly overhauled to detect signs of damage and excessive wear, and to avoid it becoming hazardous.

- Never use equipment with wet hands or near the water supply.

- Check that the appliance is correctly earthed. Most are fitted with an earth wire. Some continental equipment does not have an earth wire, but the sign ▣ indicates that the metal frame is double earthed.

Methods of Permanent Hair Removal

There are three forms of electrical, permanent, hair removal:

- **galvanic** treatment;
- the **diathermy** method; (sometimes referred to as short wave or radio wave)
- a combination of galvanic and short-wave treatments, referred to in the USA as the **Blend** method.

Originally, the term 'electrolysis' was used in relation to galvanic treatment and the term 'epilation' was used for short-wave treatment, but more recently 'electrology' has been used to relate generally to any form of electrical removal of unwanted hair.

The Galvanic Method

As has been previously indicated, this is by far the oldest of the three methods. Some of the earliest experiments in galvanism showed that the application of a direct electrical current to a solution of water caused the salt and the water to break into their constituent chemical elements, which then quickly arranged themselves to form entirely new substances. This is the process known in science as electrolysis. The new substances are sodium hydroxide – which we will refer to as **lye** – and two gases, hydrogen and chlorine. The gases are of very little concern to the electrologist, but the lye, which is highly caustic, is a very effective means of destruction when produced in the tiny hair follicle. This means that galvanic electrolysis is a *chemical* process rather than an electrical one.

To produce this chemical effect there must, of course, be a complete electrical circuit in the body. For the direct current to flow and achieve this circuit, the client holds a bar, which is connected to the positive side of the galvanic instrument, whilst the needle holder is connected to the negative terminal. It is important that the bar which the client holds should be covered with absorbent material previously soaked in saline solution (i.e. two tablespoonsful of common salt to a quart of water), and the client should be informed of the necessity to have a nice firm grip on the rod in order to avoid any fluctuations in the amount of current passing at any one time.

The needle is inserted into the hair follicle on the underside of the hair and the current is turned up to about 2 milliamps. The total time for the insertion of the needle will vary between ½ and 1½ minutes depending on the sturdiness of the hair being epilated. It will be seen that this is a long and laborious method of removing hairs, but it is also very effective and is still used by many practitioners on those hairs which are recalcitrant to other treatments.

Great care has to be exercised in the use of the galvanic method as scarring can easily occur. It is also more painful than the short-wave method and this is a factor which must be taken into account particularly in relation to the pain tolerance of the client.

Diathermy Method

This is by far the most commonly used form of epilation and is the one almost universally adopted now by electrologists. Whilst, in theory, diathermy is operated over a very large spectrum, for the practical purposes of electrology it has to operate within an assigned waveband of just over 27 megahertz, i.e. in the region of 27 million oscillations a second. The needle in this case becomes a kind of antenna which creates an area of influence called the high frequency field. As the high frequency current is continually changing its polarity, any substance which conducts electricity falling within the field is bound to be influenced by the oscillations. These oscillations are so fast that they produce a kind of friction in the atomic structure of the material and this friction, in turn, results in heat. In other words, diathermy is basically a heat treatment. It will be seen that the speed of these oscillations, 27 million per second, makes the diathermic method of epilation much faster than galvanism. The length of time that the needle is actually in the follicle will depend on the dampness of the follicle itself and on the intensity of the current used, but, assuming that the instrument used is one of the transistorised types with a setting of between 1 and 2, the time involved is merely how long it takes to press the switch button on and off.

The Blend Method

This is an effective way of dealing with the coarser hairs that are always resistant to treatment. In short, this is a method which combines galvanism and diathermy in the same needle so that they can be used separately or together in various formulations. The Blend method is used primarily in the USA.

Chapter 6

CONSULTATIONS

Consultations are of vital importance to both the electrologist and the client, and especially to a new client.

It is advantageous to have ready a **record card** to note various details concerning the client. There are cards available which list all the relevant details (see Fig. 12). These can be ticked off and signed by the client herself.

The question of medical treatment on the record card should be carefully examined as clients are sometimes unaware that hormone treatment for various complaints could be the reason for their hypertrichosis.

Many potential clients become nervous when contemplating electrology treatment. They are encouraged when professional expertise is displayed by the electrologist, with a well-groomed appearance, and an authoritative and efficient manner. Perhaps most importantly, a sympathetic understanding of the emotional stress that the client may be suffering, due to the embarrassing problem of unwanted hair, should be offered. It is essential that the client is able to rely on a scrupulously clean clinic and sterile tools and equipment, tended with hygienic care.

It is reasonable to allow thirty minutes for the first visit, some twelve to fifteen minutes of which may be allocated to the consultation and the remaining fifteen minutes for treatment of the client if she decides to start straightaway. When in the clinic it is better to start treatment at once rather than allowing 'cold feet' to postpone treatment.

It should be explained to the client that although this treatment is a permanent cure it is progressive and each hair has to

NAME				DOCTOR			
ADDRESS				ADDRESS			
				TEL.			
TEL. HOME WORK				MEDICAL TREATMENT			
PREVIOUS EPIL. SCARRING				AGE SEX			
SKIN CONDITION							
HAIR CONDITION							
MEDICAL HISTORY							
HEART		BLOOD			ASTHMA		
LIVER		KIDNEYS			HEPATITIS		
ALLERGIES							
		CLIENT'S SIGNATURE			DATE		

DATE	TREATMENT COMMENTS	CURRENT INTENSITY	NEEDLE SIZE	DATE	TREATMENT COMMENTS	CURRENT INTENSITY	NEEDLE SIZE

Repeated on reverse and continuation cards

Fig. 12 A Record Card

be treated separately. The hairs will gradually become fewer
and more interspersed. All interference by the client must
stop, especially plucking. *Do not* give an estimation of the expected duration of the treatments necessary to kill all the hair.

This is a difficult estimation – the client could be bitterly disappointed if the prediction is wrong and her faith in the operator and the treatment itself will be shattered.

An explanation of the treatment is helpful to the client as so many people have a fear of injections. It must be explained that a needle or probe is used, that it is inserted into an opening which is already present, and that no discomfort is felt until the probe is charged with electrical current, when she will experience a sensation similar to a slight sting. This sensation is more noticeable in certain areas where there are more nerve endings, such as the centre of the upper lip and the skin at the centre underneath the lower lip.

Contra-indications to Electrology

During the initial consultation with the client it is important to ascertain knowledge of any signs or conditions that would contra-indicate treatment. Any doubt as to the health or condition of the client would preclude electrology treatment. Checks must be made before treatments are applied. If the client is receiving medical treatment, then approval must be obtained before any further treatments are contemplated. This is in the interest of all concerned and is an essential part of professional practice.

The following guide lists some of the contra-indications to electrology treatment.

- Areas of inflammation, cuts, sores or open wounds.
- Any abnormal skin condition.
- Signs of infectious disease.
- Hairy moles.
- Women in the final months of pregnancy. They should not be treated, not because there would be harm to the unborn child, but because hair which appears to coarsen particu-

larly on the abdomen and breasts during pregnancy, often disappears after the birth of the child.

- Clients who are emotionally disturbed. They have a pain threshold which is usually too low to tolerate any discomfort. It is better to co-ordinate electrology treatment with other medical treatment the client might be receiving.

- Young people under the age of sixteen years. They should not be treated except in circumstances agreed with the client's doctor, since many hormonal imbalances correct themselves as the youngster matures.

- Clients suffering from diabetes, epilepsy, heart conditions, asthma, blood pressure problems, hepatitis, venereal diseases or hormone imbalances. They should only be treated with the consent of their doctors. Clients suffering from diabetes tend to have slow skin-healing properties and are susceptible to infection.

  Epileptic attacks might be triggered by the sensation of the needle probing as it enters the follicle.

  Sufferers from heart conditions seldom offer problems but the doctor's consent is best sought and obtained.

  Asthmatic clients who have a nervous disposition should only be treated with their doctor's permission and advice as to how to handle the client in the possible event of an attack occurring during treatment.

  On no account should a needle used on a client suffering from hepatitis be used on another client. This disease can be transferred from client to client in the event of the needles being carelessly, or ineffectively, sterilised. (This matter is referred to in the next chapter.) This also applies to those suffering from venereal disease and AIDS.

- People receiving medical treatment. They must not receive other treatment from the electrologist. It is neither ethical nor safe to do so without the consent and guidance of the client's doctor.

- Those displaying abnormal fear of the treatment. They must be carefully handled: only when a client has had the treatment fully explained and has accepted what is entailed should treatment be attempted. The confidence and co-operation of the client is essential for the treatment's success.

This list of contra-indications appears at first sight to be formidable, but it must not deter the electrologist. Many of the conditions listed, while contra-indicating treatment, will be treatable after checking and clearing with the client's doctor.

Chapter 7

PROCEDURE FOR GENERAL TREATMENT

Before commencing treatment the importance of the **sterilisation** of the needles to be used, and the processes involved, must be clearly understood. It has now been recognised that the usual method used by salons – holding the needle for several seconds in a ball of cotton-wool soaked in surgical spirit and turning the setting of the machine to its maximum strength – is not sufficient to ensure that the needles are completely sterilised. The main source of concern lies with cross-infection of hepatitis and other germs, which can be carried by a client although neither suffering from nor exhibiting symptoms of the disease. Needles are safe to use if they have been heated to 200 °C (392 °F).

A small, new sterilisation unit has recently been introduced to solve this problem – it is simple to use as the needles are placed in a small opening containing glass beads and then heated, as described in Chapter 8. A second method to ensure complete safety for the client is to use sterile needles which are individually packed and used for one treatment only. This method does become expensive; however, ideally the use of a new, unused, sterile needle, or a sterile disposable needle, is to be recommended as essential. Clinical sterilisation methods may be cheaper, but storing them becomes a problem and cannot be as effective as the ready-to-use, disposable or sterile needle. A third method for metal equipment is the autoclave sterilisation machine usually employed in the medical field.

First of all ensure that the client is seated comfortably, either in a suitable chair or on a couch, and that the part of the client which is to be treated is in a good light. If a cold-light magnifier is being used, then this should be positioned so that it is approximately over the area which is to be treated and at a good working distance for the electrologist. Make a point of washing your hands in such a way that the client is aware that you are doing so, then seat yourself comfortably alongside the client. It is important that your back is not strained as many operators develop strained necks and tense shoulders because of bad working positions.

Fig. 13 The Working Position

The area of the skin to be treated should be thoroughly cleansed with a mild antiseptic. Hibitane and surgical spirit are probably the most common, and the best used. Select a needle: 003, 004 and 005 are the sizes which are used on the face, depending on the thickness of the hair. The 003 needles are used on the very fine hair on the upper lip of female clients – these needles are very delicate and must be carefully handled.

Depending on the length of the treatment, the operator and the client must decide which hairs should be treated first. It is advisable to choose only some of the hairs of a group, making sure that they are well spaced. If hairs are epilated too closely together, inflammation and soreness may be experienced.

In order to gauge the depth of the hair follicle, hold a hair with the tweezers as close to the epidermis as possible and tease out the hair. The distance between where the root sheath ends and the points of the tweezers indicates the depth of the sebaceous gland. Where the epidermis is thin this length of hair is about a quarter of the entire root length, and in thick epidermal areas it is about half the entire root length.

This test acts as a guideline as to the depth of insertion required to epilate hairs properly. The process is likely to be most effective when the hairs chosen are at the anagen, active, growth stage. It is difficult to recognise which stage of growth the hair is in by merely looking at it. Even when epilating a hair with its root sheath intact, which indicates the anagen growth stage, it cannot be assumed that the neighbouring hair also is anagen. It is important that the papilla, the germinal matrix

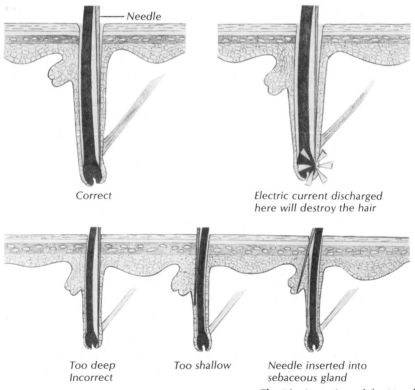

Correct

Electric current discharged here will destroy the hair

Too deep Incorrect

Too shallow

Needle inserted into sebaceous gland

Fig. 14 Insertion of the Needle

and the germinating cell area of the hair bulb are destroyed for the successful, easy and permanent epilation of the hair.

Having established the expected length of the anagen hair follicle, the needle (or probe, as some clients prefer it to be called) is carefully inserted into the hair follicle. The probe should slide under the hair at the same angle as its growth and if there is any discomfort the probe is being inserted incorrectly (see Fig. 14). The method should always be to probe gently, with the fingers stretching the skin to allow the needle to slip into the hair follicle.

The button on the foot control should be pressed or set for the 'working point' which can be tolerated by the client. This can only be determined by starting with a low current strength and gradually working up to what the client can actually tolerate. The 'point' should therefore be at the setting which is the maximum the client can bear and the minimum epilation time required to slide the hair out of the follicle, and most important of all at a level which will not cause the surface of the skin any damage. The sensitivity of the client's skin must also be taken into consideration.

Most clients are able to tolerate fifteen to thirty minutes treatment, but it is vital to explain that treatments on the same area should be spaced every fourteen days to allow the skin to heal completely, both on the surface and in the inner aspect of the epidermis.

The treated area should be cleansed again and covered with an antiseptic cream or lotion. The client must, if possible, refrain from using make-up for four hours and, if agreeable, for twenty-four hours – tinted calamine lotions are available instead. The client should also be told that infection is very often caused by dust and by dirty fingers which are tempted to touch and scratch the tender areas, – and that cleanliness is therefore essential.

If there is redness or slight swelling on the upper lip, witchhazel compresses are very soothing. If by any chance small scabs appear which look like little red dots, they should be

allowed to disappear by themselves, as with the crust formation of any injury. Scratching and 'picking off' nature's healing
patterns can result in scarring of the epidermis.

It has been found that oily skins usually heal better with a drier
type of lotion, like calamine, and that dry and normal skins
respond to an oilier treatment, such as an antiseptic cream.

Reactions against Treatment

In case of incorrect treatment, the electrologist must recognise
the various reactions which can occur and also understand why
they occur.

Swelling

The most common reasons for swelling are over-insertion,
allergies to galvanic current and too great a concentration of
work in one area. There are some cases when a reaction is
caused merely by the insertion of something into the hair
follicle, but this is unusual. A coating of antiseptic cream and the
application of an ice-cold pack helps to alleviate swelling.

White Circles Around the Hair Follicles

These mean that the hair has been overtreated and the epidermis is actually burned, that the insertion has been too
shallow, or that the hand of the operator has been unsteady.
These rings will heal, but the damage *must not* occur again – it
takes several weeks for the tissue to renew itself.

Crusts (Blood or Lymph)

These are also caused by new treatment, so they must be
allowed to fall off by themselves or pitting and scarring will
occur.

Bruising or Bleeding

A bad probe insertion, and bent or blunt needles, can be the cause of bruising or bleeding. Bad insertions will not be tolerated by the client, or by an examiner, so the probe insertion is one of the first important lessons to be learned.

Scarring or Stippling

If scarring or stippling of the skin occurs in some clients it may be due to one, or a combination, of the following causes:

- operating too quickly;
- using a faulty machine;
- using a bent, blunt needle;
- using a needle which is too short or hooked;
- using a current which is too strong;
- concentrating the treatment too much in one area;
- introducing the needle into the hair follicle at the wrong angle;
- switching the electric current on at the moment the needle touches the skin and keeping it on until it is withdrawn.

Chapter 8

THE ELECTROLOGY CLINIC

As electrology is an invasive technique, i.e. an instrument is used to pass through the skin, it is in many ways similar to minor surgery. Accordingly, the electrology clinic should present a clinical appearance.

Equipment

Instruments

The epilation instruments are, of course, the most important pieces of equipment. They are usually available in two forms, a portable form and a clinical form.

Obviously the portable form has advantages where the electrologist has a visiting practice as well as a static one, because

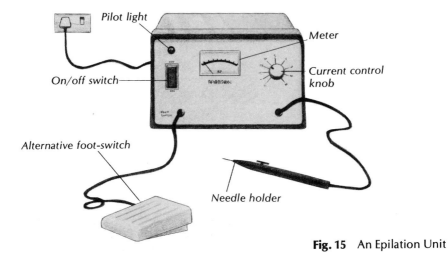

Fig. 15 An Epilation Unit

the portable units are smaller and lighter, and are invariably fitted with a carrying handle. On the other hand, the clinical model is usually much more impressive and in a clinic which depends on one instrument it is worthwhile considering the visual effect on the client. Clients tend, quite wrongly of course, to equate efficiency and expertise with the type of equipment which the therapist manipulates, and if this is large and impressive and has a number of lights and meters this invariably impresses the majority of clients. It should, however, be pointed out that internally most of the portable and clinical units are identical, i.e. they produce the same form of current with the same kind of intensity. In fact, in many cases, the works are absolutely identical, except that in a clinical model they are put in a much more impressive casing, sometimes with the addition of extra lights and meters.

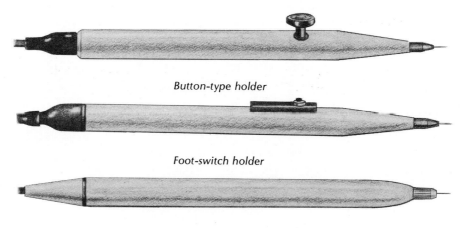

Button-type holder

Foot-switch holder

Switch-controlled holder

Fig. 16   Needle Holders

Trolley

The trolley on which to put the instrument should be either plastic or metal because of the ease of sterilisation. Wooden trolleys are not easy to sterilise and therefore should be avoided.

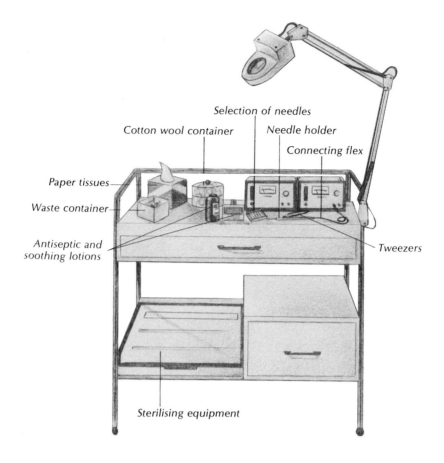

Selection of needles

Cotton wool container   Needle holder

Connecting flex

Paper tissues

Waste container

Antiseptic and
soothing lotions

Tweezers

Sterilising equipment

Fig. 17   A Typical Trolley Layout

Magnifying Light

The magnifying light – the light source of the magnifier –
should be cold light, i.e. fluorescent tube, because this may be
used near to the client's skin without causing any discomfort,
whereas the tungsten-bulb type produces considerable heat
even with a small output bulb, and this can become uncomfort-
able to the client in time. There are available magnifiers with a
straightforward magnifying lens and ones which have a second
lens of greater power (usually a 15 diopter lens) inserted into
them. In the latter case the large lens gives a general indication

of the whole area, whilst the 15 diopter lens increases considerably the magnification of the smaller area under actual treatment.

The magnifying light may be free-standing, clamped to a trolley, or wall-mounted.

Fig. 18   An Illuminated Magnifier

Steriliser

The choice of steriliser lies between the vapour type and the ultraviolet type. It is generally considered that the ultraviolet type will keep instruments sterile as long as they have been well sterilised before being put into the cabinet. The vapour type, on the other hand, will act on instruments which are not completely sterile when they are put into the cabinet and would therefore appear to be the first choice for the electrologist. Moreover, the vapour type of cabinet is also usually considerably cheaper than the ultraviolet type. Whilst these sterilisers may be used for instruments and materials applicable to the surface of the skin they are not an acceptable form of sterilisation for the needles. Except when a new, pre-packed, sterilised needle is used for each client, all needles should be treated in the glass-bead type steriliser. In practice, after switching on the instrument twenty minutes should be allowed for stabilisation and a further ten minutes to complete the process. Instruments may vary, however, and it is wise to follow the manufacturer's instructions.

Fig. 19 A Bead Steriliser

Other Equipment

To complete the equipment the electrologist will also require a couple of small stainless-steel bowls or dishes, a small stainless-steel tray on which the needle holder can be placed when not actually being used, a pedal-operated waste bin and a couple of closed-top jars to contain such items as cotton wool, such jars are available in glass with chrome-plated lids which have rubber seals. Tweezers have been deliberately omitted from this list of equipment because most electrologists tend to use the type of tweezers with which they were trained. The clinic should of course have hot and cold running water.

Under a law passed in 1982, all clinics using invasive (skin-piercing) techniques in England and Wales are required to register their premises with the local health authority. This includes acupuncture, tattooing, ear-piercing and electrology.

Furnishings

Seating for the Client

There are at least three possible choices of seating for the client.

A Beauty-type Chair
This, of course, is excellent for the treatment of faces but not so convenient when dealing with other parts of the body.

Fig. 20(a)   A Beauty Chair–Upright

Fig. 20(b)   A Beauty Chair–Extended

A Treatment Couch with Tilt Head
This enables the therapist to work on the face as well as on the legs and body in general. It is not, however, as comfortable as a beauty chair.

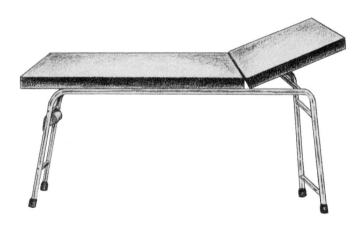

Fig. 21   A Tubular Treatment Couch with Tilt Head

A Combination Chair/Couch

The kind of chair which converts into a couch has very obvious advantages. It looks designed for the purpose, which of course impresses the client. It is very comfortable for face or neck and shoulder treatments and it may be levelled out for bikini-line and leg treatments. When in the upright position it takes up a minimum of space, which is a consideration when working in a small room or cubicle. Such combination chair/couches are usually available in a variety of colours – electrologists' most popular choice is white because of its clinical appearance.

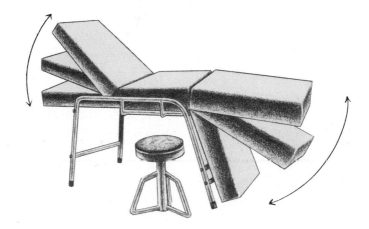

Fig. 22 A Combination Chair/Couch

Seating for the Therapist

To complete the furniture of the electrology room or clinic, an adjustable stool is necessary for the therapist. These are normally available in two forms – the revolving type and the 'gas' type. The principle of the revolving type is well known. The gas type is easier to operate in that by releasing a lever it automatically comes up to the level required. These again are available in a variety of colours so one would choose a stool to match the colour of the couch or chair being used.

The Hygiene of the Clinic

It is impossible to exaggerate the importance of strict hygiene wherever an invasive technique is involved because penetration of the skin provides easy access for pathological organisms of all types. It is therefore important to sterilise not only the skin being treated, but also everything that is likely to come into contact with the client.

This means that the epilation machine must be carefully and thoroughly cleaned, and disinfected with a suitable liquid disinfectant. The same applies to the trolley, the magnifier, and any other items. Stainless-steel bowls and glass containers must be washed thoroughly and disinfected.

As has been said before, needles must be sterile before using on each client. It is a good idea to have a selection of needles available, more than one of each size, so that when one has been used it can then be sterilised for at least three-quarters of an hour before using again. Packets of sterile needles must be unbroken, and this also applies to the disposable type.

Ointments must only be applied with a sterile spatula.

The electrologist must have scrupulously clean and well-manicured hands and fingernails, with no jewellery on the hands and wrists and only well-laundered overalls should be worn. If deodorants, body lotions or perfumes are to be worn, it is important that they should not be intrusive, overpowering, or other than subtle.

In conclusion, to paraphrase a famous saying 'sterilisation should not only be done, it should be seen to be done'. In other words, not only should the clinic be as completely sterile as possible, but also some of the processes should be carried out in front of the client for confidence to be assured.

UK Electrology Examining Bodies

International Therapy Examination Council (I.T.E.C.)
16 Avenue Place, Harrogate, N. Yorkshire HG2 7PJ

British Association of Beauty Therapy and Cosmetology
Suite 5, Wolseley House, Oriel Road, Cheltenham, Glos.

British Association of Electrolysists
6 Quakers Mede, Haddenham, Bucks. HP17 8EB

The City and Guilds of London Institute
46 Britannia Street, London WC1 9RE

The Institute of Electrolysis
251 Seymour Grove, Manchester M16 0DS

National Federation of Health and Beauty Therapists
P.O. Box 36, Arundel, West Sussex BN18 0SW

UK Suppliers of Electrology Equipment

George Solly Organisation Ltd.
James House, Queen Street, Henley-on-Thames, Oxon. RG9 1DF
(Tel.: 0491 577928)

Taylor Reeson Laboratories Ltd.
Carlton House, Commerce Way, Lancing, Sussex
(Tel.: 0903 761100)

Du-Lac Epilation Equipment
1 Albion Villas, The Leas, Folkestone CT20 1RP
(Tel.: 0303 54431)

Ellison
Crondal Road, Exhall, Coventry, CV7 9NH
(Tel.: 0203 361619)

INDEX